TAN DUN

EIGHT MEMORIES
IN WATERCOLOR

FOR GUITAR DUO
Transcribed by Manuel Barrueco

This arrangement was created by Manu
for the Beijing Guitar Duo.
A recording by the Duo,
Meng Su and Yameng Wang,
is available from Tonar Music
tonarmusic.com

The original version for solo piano was premiered
by Lang Lang on April 12, 2003
at the Kennedy Center, Washington D.C.
and recorded live at his November 7, 2003
Carnegie Hall recital by Deutsche Grammophon
(Schirmer edition ED 4186 - HL50485502)

ED 4564
First Printing: July 2014

ISBN: 978-1-4803-9530-5

G. SCHIRMER, Inc.

DISTRIBUTED BY

HAL•LEONARD®
CORPORATION
7777 W. BLUEMOUND RD. P.O. BOX 13819 MILWAUKEE, WI 53213

halleonard.com
musicsalesclassical.com

EIGHT MEMORIES IN WATERCOLOR

TAN DUN
transcribed by Manuel Barrueco

1. Missing Moon

Adagio con dolore

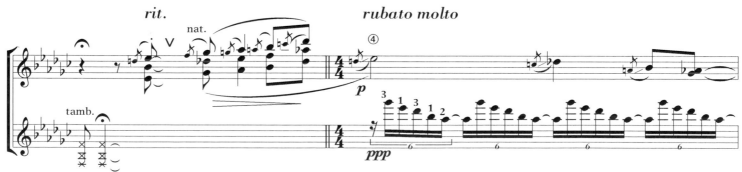

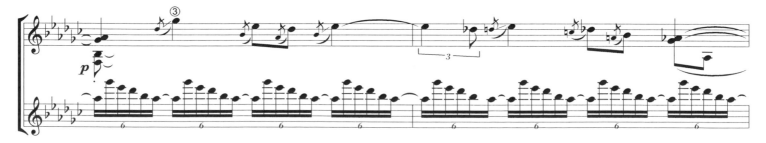

*: In performance, guitarists may alternate between part assignment after each movement for ease of tuning.

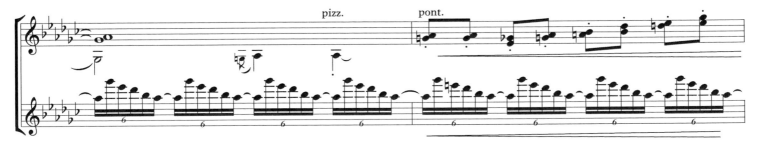

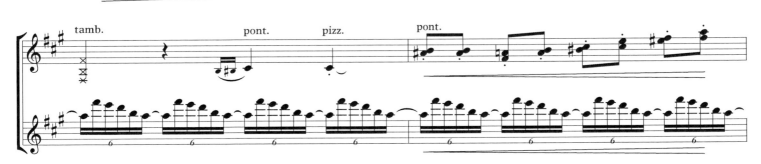

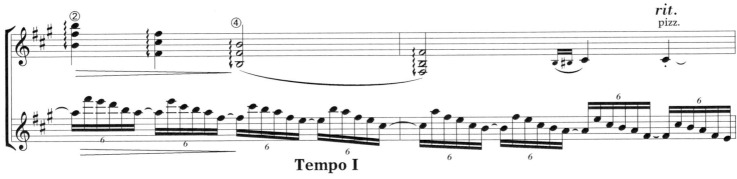

Tempo I

4

2. Staccato Beans

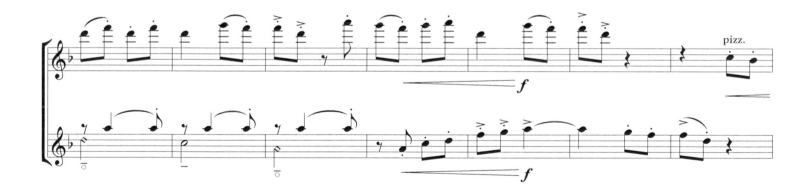

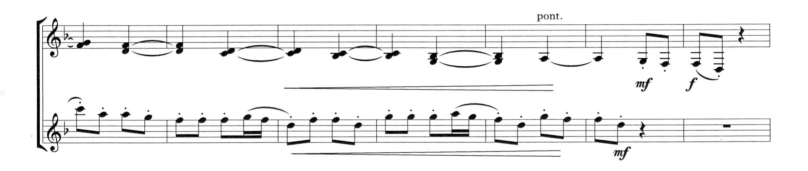

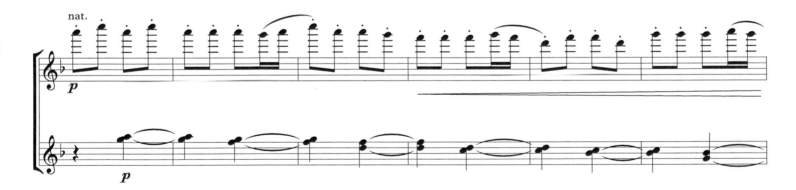

3. Herdboy's Song

Larghetto pastorale

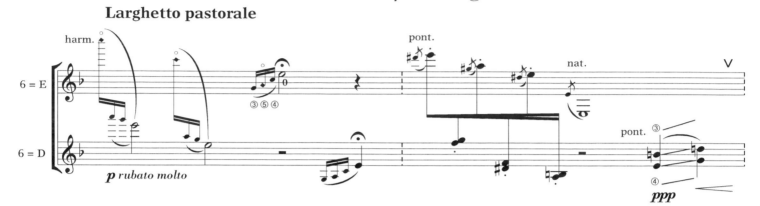

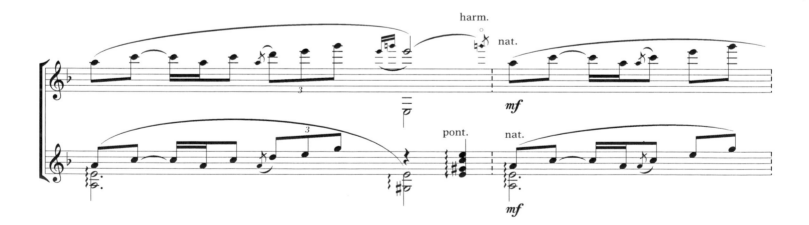

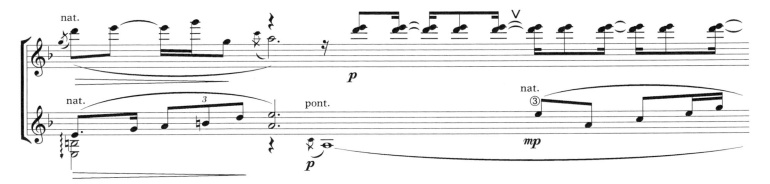

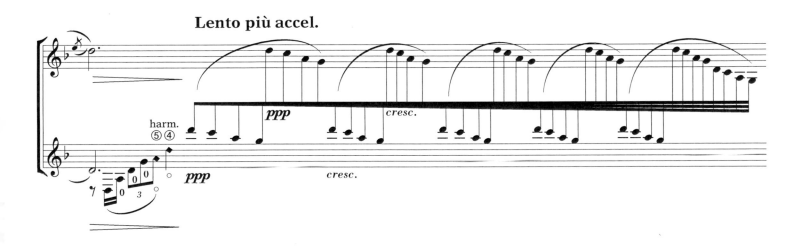

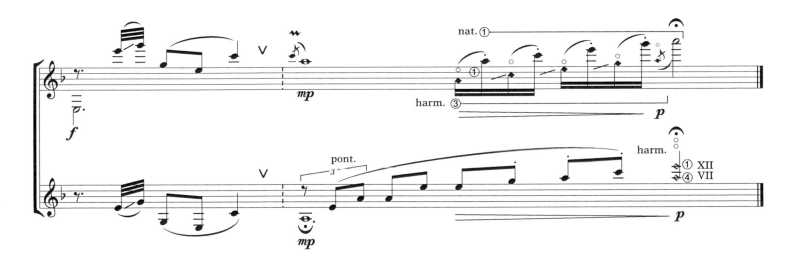

4. Blue Nun

5. Red Wilderness

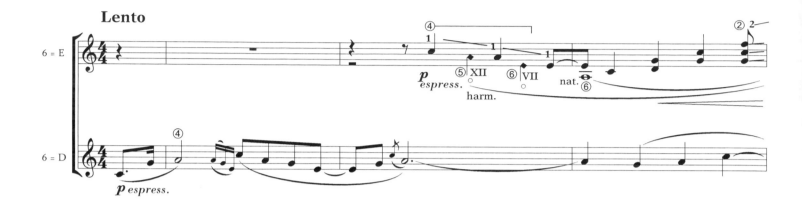

TAN DUN

EIGHT MEMORIES IN WATERCOLOR

FOR GUITAR DUO
Transcribed by Manuel Barrueco

This arrangement was created by Manuel Barrueco
for the Beijing Guitar Duo.
A recording by the Duo,
Meng Su and Yameng Wang,
is available from Tonar Music
tonarmusic.com

The original version for solo piano was premiered
by Lang Lang on April 12, 2003
at the Kennedy Center, Washington D.C.
and recorded live at his November 7, 2003
Carnegie Hall recital by Deutsche Grammophon
(Schirmer edition ED 4186 - HL50485502)

ED 4564
First Printing: July 2014

ISBN: 978-1-4803-9530-5

G. SCHIRMER, Inc.

DISTRIBUTED BY

HAL•LEONARD®
CORPORATION
7777 W. BLUEMOUND RD. P.O. BOX 13819 MILWAUKEE, WI 53213

halleonard.com
musicsalesclassical.com

EIGHT MEMORIES IN WATERCOLOR

TAN DUN

transcribed by Manuel Barrueco

1. Missing Moon

Adagio con dolore

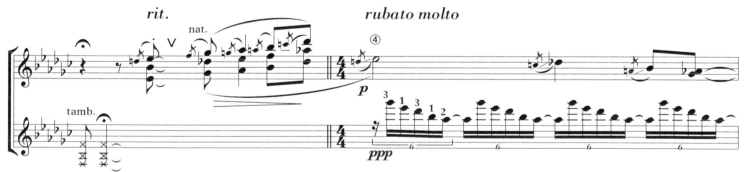

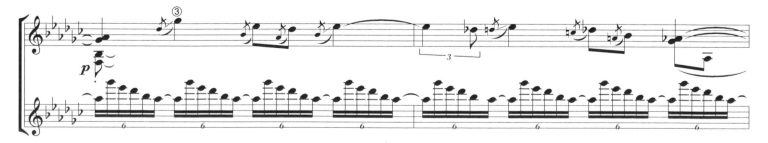

*: In performance, guitarists may alternate between part assignment after each movement for ease of tuning.

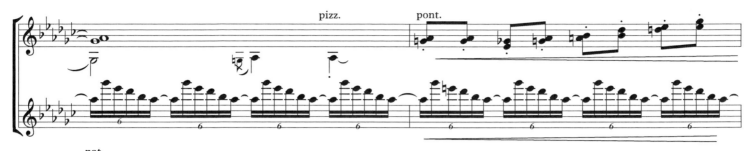

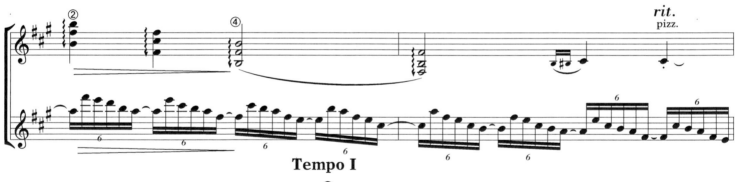

Tempo I

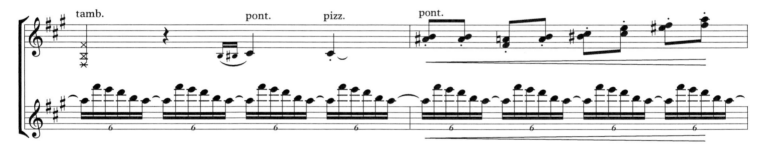

4

2. Staccato Beans

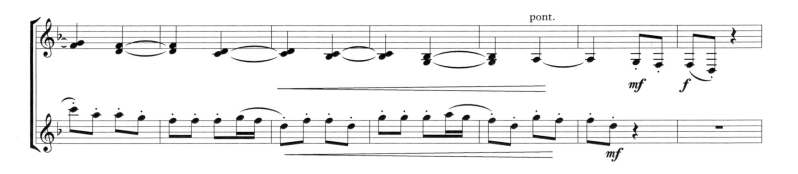

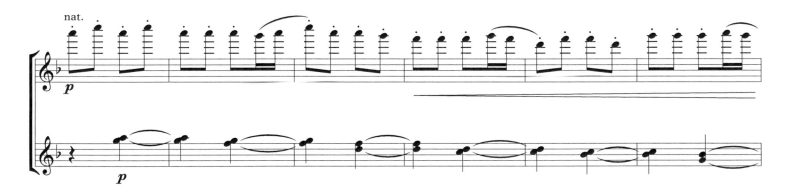

3. Herdboy's Song

Larghetto pastorale

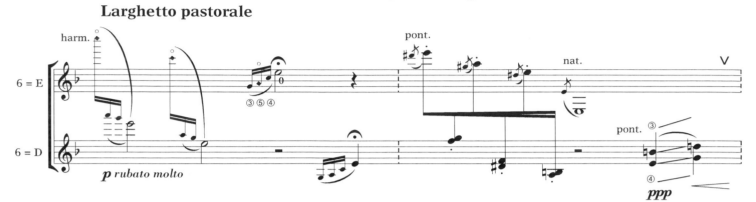

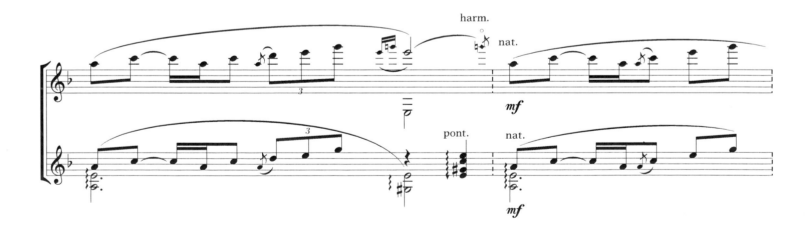

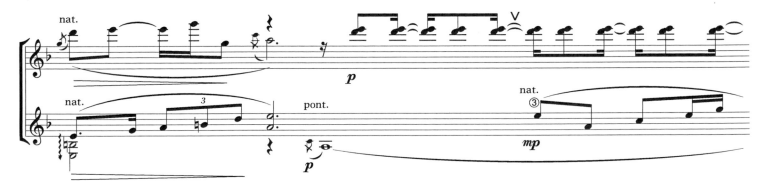

Lento più accel.

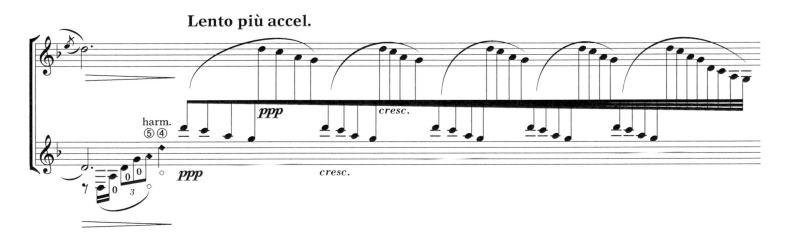

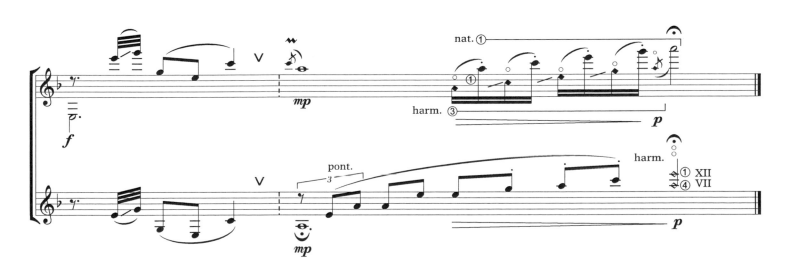

4. Blue Nun

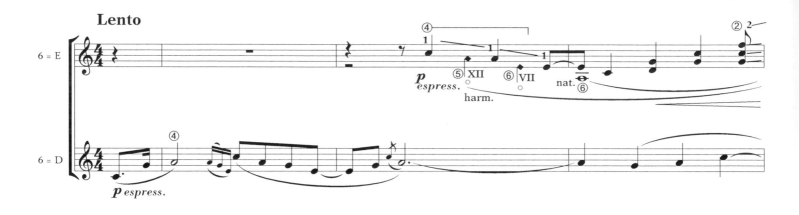

5. Red Wilderness

10

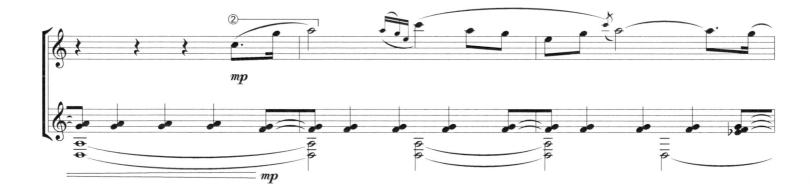

accel.   *più mosso energico*

rit. e dim. poco a poco

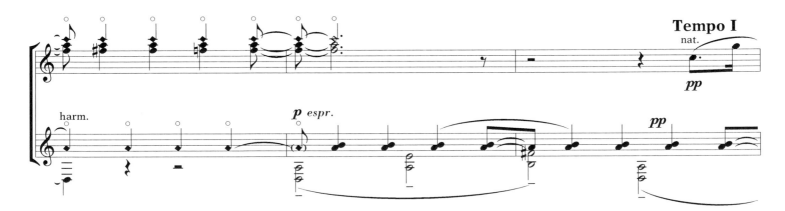

Tempo I

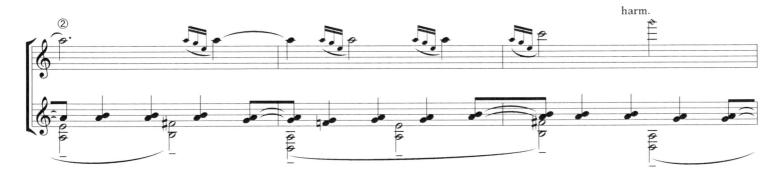

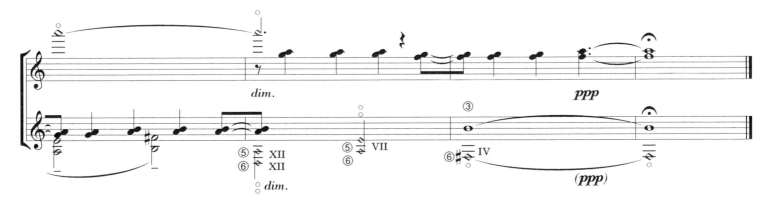

6. Ancient Burial

Adagio funebre

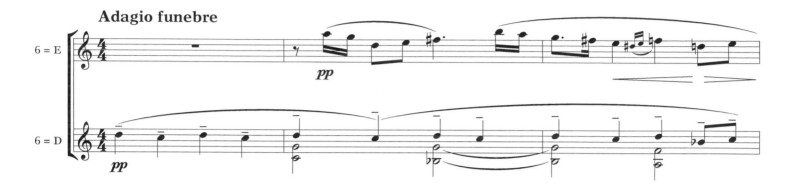

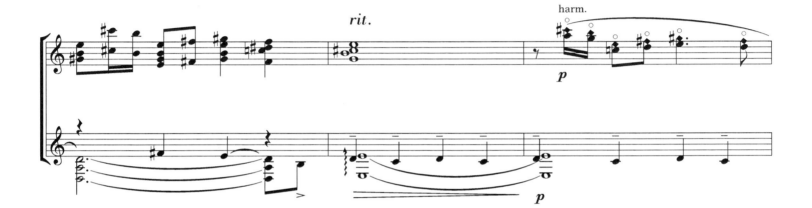

Tempo I

7. Floating Clouds

rit. e dim. poco a poco

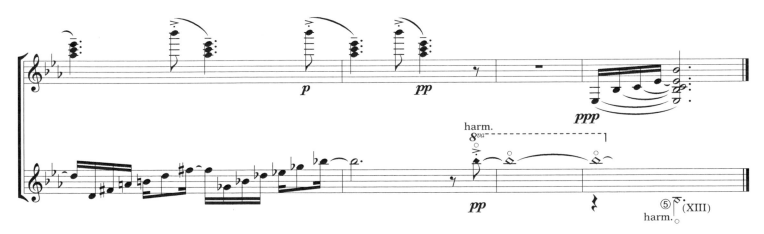

8. Sunrain

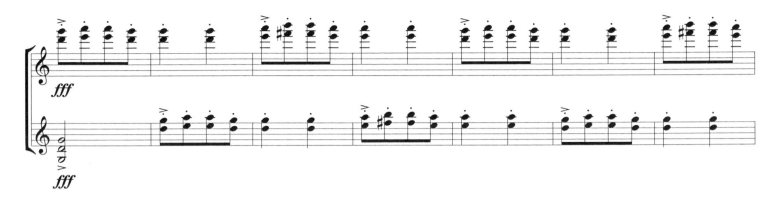

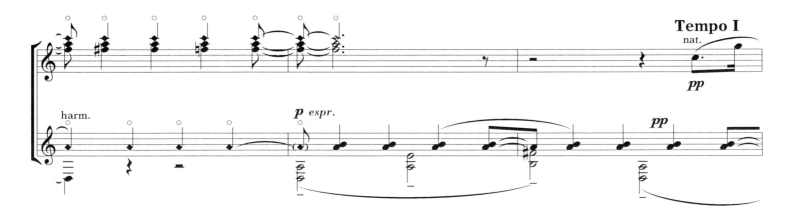

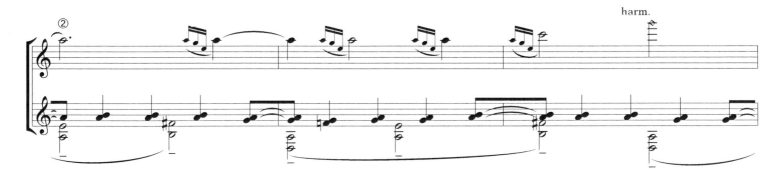

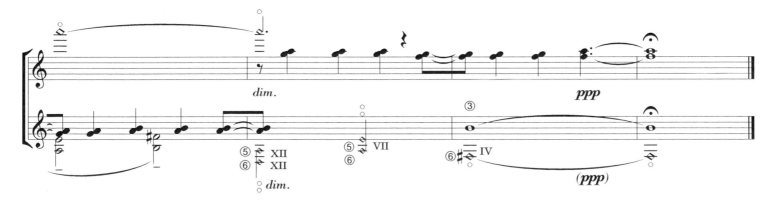

6. Ancient Burial

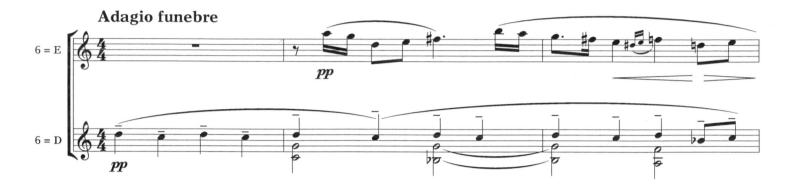

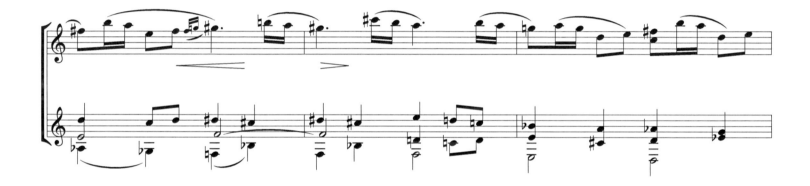

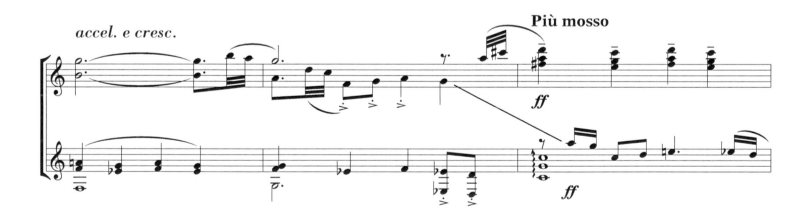

Tempo I

7. Floating Clouds

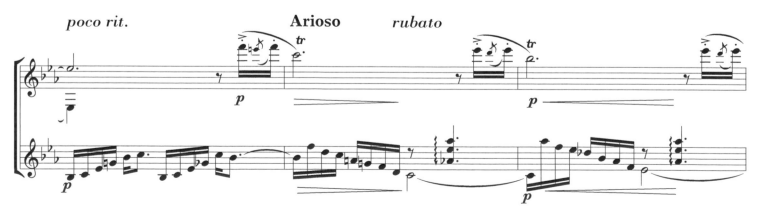

rit. e dim. poco a poco

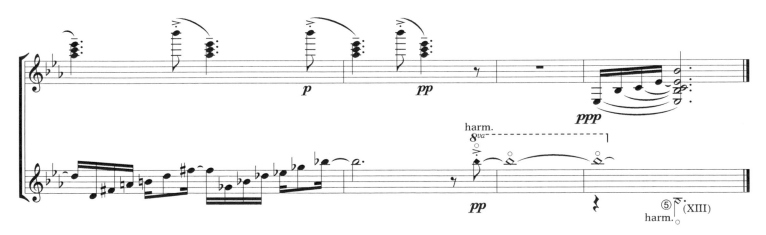

8. Sunrain

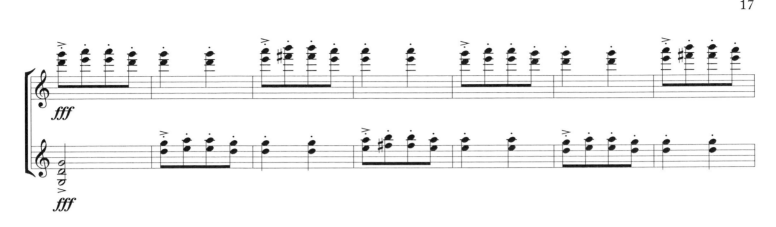